#IAMHANNAH

Giving Birth to a Generational Revolution

Teesha Boozer

Arise Publishing, LLC

Copyright © 2021 Arise Publishing, LLC

All rights reserved

The characters and events portrayed in this book are fictitious. Any similarity to real persons, living or dead, is coincidental and not intended by the author.

No part of this book may be reproduced, or stored in a retrieval system, or transmitted in any form or by any means, electronic, mechanical, photocopying, recording, or otherwise, without express written permission of the publisher.

ISBN-13: 9781736484401 (e-book)
ISBN-13: 9781736484418 (paperback)

All scripture in this book is New King James Version, copyright 1982 by Thomas Nelson, unless otherwise noted.

Front and Back Cover design by: Justin Brewer

Dedication

This is dedicated to my Lord and Savior Jesus Christ. He is the reason this book exists. Jesus - every word, every person this will touch, let it bring Glory and Honor to Your name. I love You with the everlasting love You have given me. Thanks for the empowerment, Your loving daughter forever, Teesha.

Secondly, I dedicate this book to my Husband, Troy Boozer. You have loved me in so many ways, just as Christ loved the church. Thank you for being in my corner. Let's do eternity together, always and forever your wife, Tee!

CONTENTS

Title Page
Copyright
Dedication

Forward
Chapter 1	6
Chapter 2	11
Chapter 3	15
Chapter 4	19
Chapter 5	22
Chapter 6	25
Chapter 7	29
Chapter 8	34
Chapter 9	39
Chapter 10	43
Closing Prayer	46

ACKNOWLEDGEMENTS

Thanks so much to all of you, for your encouragement and support.

To my parents Rayfield and Deborah Turner – You are my rock. You are always there for me and willing to tell the truth. Thanks for your love and support.

To my children - Jazmyne and Zaria Boozer – Thanks for your love, encouragement and support

To my besties Hanna Atiase and Rosetta Singleton – Your friendship and encouragement are priceless to me. Thanks for all the prayers and support. Love you eternally

To my friends Stacia Odums and Sharon Barnes – Thanks for your laughter and friendship. You encouraged me to keep going.

To my Pastors Glenn and Emily Walters - thanks for your support and for being Kingdom Pastors!

To Apostle Dottie Evans - your prayers and support in secret be rewarded to you openly in this season

To the intercessors and those at FireHouse – Thanks for all your prayers and support

FORWARD

In the book #IAmHannah, Teesha Boozer walks us through pursuing our purpose unrelentingly by way of Intimacy with God through Prayer. Teesha is a prayer warrior and has lived it out loud in her home, church, ministry and life! I loved reading the God inspired words Teesha penned through the life of Hannah. This book will challenge you to look within and take inventory of promises you may have let dry up and become barren, because of years of unanswered prayers. Teesha reminds us to never give up, just as Hannah never gave up, because anything that has great destiny will require great perseverance and prayer! This is an easy read yet challenging to those who God has called to Content for Change in our World. As you walk through this book, I pray the heart of a prayer warrior seeps out of these pages into your everyday life.

Emily Walters

Co-Pastor Judah Church and Director of Shabbach Youth Conferences, Charlotte NC

◆ ◆ ◆

Intro

A Generational Revolutionist –

I want to welcome you to change. This book is for those who have contended for change in an area of life for a long period of time. Maybe you have been contending for change for a loved one or friend. No matter what stand you are taking, have faith this is the time for you to see it manifest! The fact that you picked up this book, I believe, is a prophetic indicator that God has called you to this new era in your life. Amid the chaos of the world, you have been appointed to win right now! That means your dreams, passions and pursuits have not been forgotten. They are very much on the Lord's heart and He is ready to see you fulfill them all.

As you read this book, I want you to lean in. Lean into the heart of the Father concerning your situation. Every person is unique. Although this book is written to the masses, it is specifically for you. You are a called out one; this means you have been destined to give birth to something that will have an impact on your generation and the generations to come.

Let's define what I mean when I say, Generational Revolutionist. When this word came to me,

I thought of people who have reformed a nation or generation. When you look in the word of God, those who truly changed the course of a nation or the thinking of a people group had life journeys that were a precursor to the change God was ordaining. Jesus is a great example of a life written by God. God spoke of His son and His life through out the Old Testament. The prophets wrote His life and even predicted His death. When Jesus came to earth, He lived the life written of Him in scripture. Jesus' mission was to redeem and reform. His reform eliminated a religious and ritualistic mindset of the Kingdom of God. His teachings were different than all His predecessors in that He spoke to the heart of a situation and not just the actions. In the bible, we see Jesus teaching the "Beatitudes." They begin in Matthew Chapters 5-7 and He continues with his teachings with parables throughout the scriptures. Through the many teachings and parables, Jesus causes a revolution by showing the true Kingdom of God was not physical but spiritual. It is not the outward rituals of washings and burnt offerings that reveals the nature of the kingdom of God. It is out of the abundance of the Father's love for us and our love for Him that we are to live. This produces the spiritual kingdom that brings heaven to earth. Jesus brought a change of thinking that revolutionized the way we live in the kingdom today. A revolution, according to Dictionary.com, is a forcible overthrow of a government or social order, in favor of a new system. Jesus revolutionized the thinking of how the Kingdom of God truly operates and how the Kingdom of God truly comes:

Luke 17:20-21 - *Now when He was asked by the Pharisees when the kingdom of God would come, He answered them and said, "The kingdom of God does not come with observation; {21} nor will they say, 'See here!' or 'See there!' For indeed, the kingdom of God is within you."*

The Israelites were looking for a physical kingdom when God was telling them because you have Me, the Kingdom is within you. This was a revolutionary thought process that was birthed into the earth at a time of great despair due to Roman oppression. Jesus changed years of generational worship and perception in three short years.

If you have the Holy Spirit (Salvation), then you have the Kingdom within you. You have Christ within you and can do the things He did. This book was birthed to activate the generational call on your life!

Some of us have suffered long and hard. We have had ups and downs with very little evidence of victory in our lives. But, we have come into the time that those that have prayed and will continue to pray, shall see victory. #IAMHANNAH was written to help you grasp the victory you have desired to see. For some of you, it will be in business. For others, it will be for your families- changing the culture, dynamics and financial strongholds that have held them. Others will be activated in ministry. For everyone that will hold fast to prayer, you will not only have victory, but generational impact!

Being a "HANNAH" is not a gender specific role, but it is a positional place of prayer. Men can give birth supernaturally as they stand and pray about what God has placed in them. This book will show you what effectual fervent prayer does.

You are Hannah. You have experienced pain, suffering and barrenness in times past but get ready, you will see your Samuel blessing manifest. You will be impactful, and your destiny is sure. Be encourage HANNAHS, this is your time!

CHAPTER 1

Elkanah

The story of Hannah begins with the heritage of her husband, Elkanah. Elkanah was born in Ephraim. Now Ephraim was in the hill country of Palestine. He came specifically from a place called Ramathaim Zophim in Ephraim which translates, double-height of the watchers according to the Strong's Concordance. This is significant because not only was Elkanah in a high place in the hill country, he was in an even higher place, to be able to watch and see. Watchers in the Bible can refer to angels or to men on a tower who watched for the enemy on the wall. The latter is what I want to reference. When God is telling the story of your life everything is intentional -- even where you live.

Elkanah lived in a place that had a great vantage point to see far off. When praying, God desires us to be able to see what is coming:

John 16:13 "However, when He, the Spirit of truth, has come, He will guide you into all truth; for He will not speak on His own *authority,* but whatever He hears He will speak; and He will tell you things to come."

Seeing what is coming allows us to be proactive in prayer and not reactive. When we can perceive and know through the Spirit of God what lies ahead, we can bring the issue to God in prayer and receive the knowledge of how to deal with it. Elkanah lived in a place that gave him the ability to look far and wide. He could be ready at any time to sound the alarm against the enemy. As a Generational Revolutionist, it is important to realize you possess the key to the change needed in your sphere of view.

The key to the higher places of watching that unlocks spiritual insight and revelation is your relationship with God. As you fellowship in prayer (and the Word), you will begin to build the friendship that Jesus speaks of in John 15. Elkanah represents the people of God being a co-laborer in prayer through relationship and position. His position is in the high place or Ramathaim Zophaim and the relationship is in his name. Elkanah means "God has possessed" according to Strong's Concordance. This is a relationship with God that is totally taken over by the Spirit of God. This is a person willing to pray in season and out because you are totally in love with God. Your vantage point continues to increase in height as you fall more and more in-love with God, allowing Him to possess you. This possession is not something that overtakes your will, but a relationship that is mutually deemed the most important. In this, you are totally given over to God as he is already totally given over to you.

The name Ephraim means fruitful. The place of prayer is the place of fruitfulness. It is where you birth and release the ideas and impressions God has given for your personal assignment, as well as the Body of Christ (also known as the Church). We are created as the possession of God to bring His Kingdom to earth. Only through sweet communion with the Father in prayers and intercessions can we accomplish this. It is our God-given privilege to walk with Him on the earth.

Imagine yourself as Elkanah. He has called you to the double-high place of a watcher in the Kingdom. He desires for you to watch with Him to bring His Kingdom down to earth. It is in this place, this precious intimate place that the battle is won. Remember, this is not a teaching on the types of prayer. However, I want you to understand that prayer is a full-bodied place and experience in God. It includes tongue-speaking, listening, supplications, petitions, waiting in the presence, and all manner of biblical prayer being implemented. Please do not lock yourself in a box when it comes to communion with God in prayer. Be free in Him and follow His lead. Remember, you are seated in heavenly places in Christ, (Ephesians 2:6)! Take your seat in Ramathaim Zophim and begin to see from the heavenly perspective.

Prayer

Lord, I thank you for desiring me. By faith, I desire you. I want to take my seat with Christ in the High Places with God. I desire to live from the vantage point of "It is Finished" for every victory I will obtain in the earth. No longer will I not know where I sit. Today, I begin to Reign with you from the High Places through our loving relationship in Christ. I am anticipating the new places we are going together, the new heights will will conquer together, and the new breakthroughs I will see in the days, weeks, and years ahead, Amen!

CHAPTER 2

Peninnah

Peninnah was one of the wives of Elkanah. She dwelt in Ephraim and had many children, both sons and daughters. The bible indicates that Peninnah was an adversary to Hannah. Hannah was the other wife of Elkanah. She would provoke Hannah and speak proudly to her (1Sam1: 2-6) because Hannah had no children.

The Lord prompted my heart that Peninnah is a symbol of the world in which we live. She had everything anyone could want at that time. She was married, with children, and had sons to give her husband for an inheritance. Anyone in that time period would say she was fruitful. I can imagine people even envied her because of all she accomplished. In fact, her name means jewel. Like a precious jewel, the world valued her and treasured her worth. I believe this is the reason Hannah was sorely vexed (1Sam 1:6). According to the standards of people in their day, Peninnah had accomplished much; but Hannah was left lacking. We will talk about Hannah next, but I want you to notice something about Peninnah. It is hard to mention her, without mentioning Hannah. Peninnah had worth to the world but she needed Hannah, whom the world rejected, to substantiate her worth.

The enemy sees your worth. He also understands if you knew your worth, you would annihilate him. So, the enemy devises a plan against you. He adorns those that follow him with the things that you desire. He wants you to look at how "well" they are doing. The enemy is enticing you to become vexed by an ungodly lie. He is dangling a false testimony for you to accept that says you are forgotten by God, unloved and nothing you desire will come to pass. The enemy wants you to deny God and choose his testimony. Now as believers, we may not outwardly say we deny God, but we do this when we function using insecurities, hopelessness and failures in our lives that contradict the Word of God.

Peninnah is the bully of the world that says, "If God loves you, then He would......" You fill in the blank. Peninnah is the sparkling jewel (as her name indicates), that is illuminated and gazed upon by the world because she has everything.

Peninnah also represents the major thing in your life you have yet to overcome. It is the one thing you have sought God for but the one thing that seems to elude you. It is the place of your cycle of brokenness, sorrow, unbelief and wavering. You may manage these feelings for a time; then the enemy brings the jewel in front of you again. Waves of emotions flood your soul and peace eludes you. The cycle of your heart breaking again is painful and tiring. But God in His mercy comes and stills the waves of ungodly emotions once more. I am talking to those who have very legitimate requests and needs that are biblical and still.... no answer. This is the Spirit of Peninnah that comes to taunt you about what has not changed. It comes to flaunt the obvious, to oppress and keep you in the cycle. But, this book is going to set you free from the spirit of Peninnah. Let's look at Hannah and put this all together.

CHAPTER 3

Hannah

Hannah was also Elkanah's wife. But Hannah's story is different than Peninnah in that she had no children. In that day, the wife bore the blame and humiliation of not having children.

Hannah however, had one thing that Peninnah did not - the love of her husband. That means his attention, favor, grace, protection and intimacy were toward her. Hannah's life was that of a typical generational reformist. The natural life did not reflect the life God intended. Hannah's name meant favor. Yet her life did not seem to exude the favor she desired. Elkanah and Hannah also had intimacy and relationship, but there was no fruit being produced.

I can imagine the yearly family journey to Shiloh to worship was painful for Hannah (1 Sam 1:3). Peninnah would be with her children as they ran back and forth. The excitement of the journey for the children and the laughter that would ensue would bring smiles to everyone. But, Hannah was lagging in the back at a distance to avoid the jesting of Peninnah as much as possible. When they arrived in Shiloh, Elkanah would worship with offerings through the priests Hophni and Phineas. He would give portions to everyone, including the children. But to Hannah, he gave the more worthy portion or double portion, (1Sam 1:5). Hannah was doubly favored but it did not change her situation nor make it easy.

Let us pause here in the story and look at

favor. Often in the church world, something good happens and we equate that as being God's favor or God being good to us. But if something is not going our way then something must be wrong. I am not saying that is wrong all of the time; but maybe misappropriated. When thinking of favor, I often think of Mary, mother of Jesus. An angel greeted her and said,

Luke 1:28 - *And the angel came in unto her, and said, Hail, thou that art highly favored, the Lord is with thee: blessed art thou among women. (King James Version)*

Think about this, the Lord has sent his angel to tell you how favored you are, then proceeds to tell you one of the most impossible things would happen to you! You are going to have a child by the Holy Spirit? I can imagine I would say, "Who is Holy Spirit and how can I have a child?" "I'm engaged to Joseph and oh well, I guess I'll be stoned." I am joking here but can you imagine the pressure of being with child and no husband? Being favored by God, pushed Mary into a faith walk like none other. She had to trust God for the pregnancy and trust God with her life. She birthed the Savior that was a Generational Revolutionist, but the path to get there was not easy.

Hannah's journey was one of great trial. Every day she looked at her life and it did not add up to fruitfulness or favor she hoped for as a wife. Barrenness was a constant reminder as she looked at children that were by her husband but not with her. Hannah would see a jewel (Peninnah), that had everything the world could want. All that was in Hannah's hand was double the meat from an offering and the love of a husband.

CHAPTER 4

Contending for a Generation (Part I)

Yes, Hannah was having a rough go at it. The pressure of the world and its' ways were weighty. It looked as though Peninnah was thriving and Hannah was surviving. But what if that isn't the narrative at all? What if Hannah was actually thriving and Peninnah was surviving? Peninnah was in the world system, doing things the world's way and still her husband loved a childless wife more. I believe Peninnah's harassment of Hannah had little to do with Hannah and more to do with Peninnah. You see, the enemy hates the children of God. We are the light bearers and we are the ones who make a difference in the world. I believe Peninnah was miserable because she did not have her husband's full heart. To vex Hannah was to shout to Elkanah and the world that Hannah was not worth it. I am the jeweled one, look at me and love me. The world wants the you to look at it and agree with its ungodly ways. You cannot do this.

We must keep our eyes on the Father. Hannah was thriving spiritually; which is where it counts. Hannah's heart was turned toward God through the love of her husband. She learned that love was not based on circumstances. God was bringing Hannah to a place of absolute surrender because a generation was at stake. Anyone can birth children. It takes the favor of God to birth someone that will impact the nations.

When you read further into 1 Samuel, you will see that Hophni and Phineas, the two priests were wicked. They were causing Israel to sin with the offerings and sleeping with women in the temple. Eli the current judge did not correct the problem. So, God stepped in to bring about a solution. Hannah held the solution for the nation and God allowed Peninnah to prepare her.

In the body of Christ, we do not like to talk about the hard places. This was a hard place for Hannah. God did not intervene and stop Peninnah from hurting Hannah. God did not immediately come to Hannah's rescue over the years. We know it was years because Peninnah had several children. God took what the enemy meant for evil and turned into a testimony of breakthrough for Hannah.

When you have a Generational Revolution on the inside of you for a nation, the cost is greater. The price is higher because the impact will be lasting. Hannah paid a price that was greater than Peninnah. We know of Hannah's child Samuel. We do not know of Peninnah's children at all. The impact was not generational. That does not mean they were less valued. It just reveals an understanding of the why.

When you look at people in the bible that had a great impact, the testimonies of their lives were not easy. Abraham, Joseph, David and Jesus impacted generations, but their lives were not ones of roses and sunshine every day.

CHAPTER 5

Contending for a

Generation (Part II)

1 Samuel 1:10-16 - *she was deeply distressed and prayed to the Lord and wept bitterly. ¹¹ And she vowed a vow and said, "O Lord of hosts, if you will indeed look on the affliction of your servant and remember me and not forget your servant, but will give to your servant a son, then I will give him to the Lord all the days of his life, and no razor shall touch his head."*

¹² As she continued praying before the Lord, Eli observed her mouth. ¹³ Hannah was speaking in her heart; only her lips moved, and her voice was not heard. Therefore, Eli took her to be a drunken woman. ¹⁴ And Eli said to her, "How long will you go on being drunk? Put your wine away from you." ¹⁵ But Hannah answered, "No, my lord, I am a woman troubled in spirit. I have drunk neither wine nor strong drink, but I have been pouring out my soul before the Lord. ¹⁶ Do not regard your servant as a worthless woman, for all along I have been speaking out of my great anxiety and vexation." (English Standard Version)

Birthing a generational revolutionist requires prayer. Earlier we talked about being in the place of prayer in the double high place. Hannah went to God with her petition and she poured her soul before the Lord. We are in a season right now where God is igniting those that will fight with Him against the enemy for the change this generation needs. The reason it has been so hard, and so long, is that what you have in you is going to revolutionize systems, technologies, science, religion, families, regions and the list goes on. This is not limited to a Sunday morning run around the church because you gave a spot-on prophetic word. This is beyond anything you have ever experience on a personal level. Hannah NEVER experienced having children, <u>but Hannah prayed</u>. Hannah had been intimate with Elkanah before and did not conceive. <u>But Hannah prayed.</u> Hannah had never reared children. <u>But Hannah prayed.</u> We know this much about Hannah; she had enough hope to pray and make her request known to God. The Bible says that they went yearly to worship. I do not believe this was her first-time asking God for help. I do not believe this was her first time pouring out her soul. But in her consistency and her willingness to be vulnerable and look foolish to the point the priest thought she was drunk, an answer came, and the season of barrenness was over.

CHAPTER 6

The Priestly Blessing

Heb 4:14-16 - *Since then we have a great high priest who has passed through the heavens, Jesus, the Son of God, let us hold fast our confession. ⁱ⁵ For we do not have a high priest who is unable to sympathize with our weaknesses, but one who in every respect has been tempted as we are, yet without sin. ¹⁶ Let us then with confidence draw near to the throne of grace, that we may receive mercy and find grace to help in time of need.* (English Standard Version)

The Bible tells us in Hebrews 4 that our great High Priest understands us like no other. He understands our shortcomings and our whys. When we come to Jesus with our petitions, we need to be confident in our great High Priest. If we approach the Throne of Grace in faith, we will receive grace in our time of need.

Hannah approached God with the hope that her petition would be granted. She was sorely troubled and crying out to the Lord in her time of need. But there was one that was watching, one whom God had given authority to bless others. This was Eli the Priest. Eli was watching Hannah and saw her state. Whatever he saw, it looked like drunkenness to him. Eli listened to her explanation and then released this blessing over her:

1 Sam 1:17 - *Then Eli answered, "Go in peace, and the God of Israel grant your petition that you have made to him."* (English Standard Version)

Eli the Priest had the authority to release a

blessing over her because of his position before God as a Levite. How much more does our High Priest, Jesus Christ have the authority to release the Generational Blessing to revolutionize lives? Jesus is after the priestly order of Melchizedek (Hebrews 5:6). This priest has no beginning or end of days. This priesthood also had the authority of a King. Your blessing is greater than Hannah's because not only do you receive the answer to your petition, but you also receive the authority to enforce it. Jesus as your High Priest has given you everything you need to enforce the generational changes that He put into you to birth.

I want to encourage you in this, sometimes things have become so common because we have dealt with them so long. The cycle of pain comes and goes in waves because the Peninnah Spirit is vexing us to kill our dreams. But God has commissioned you to go and birth this great revolution of change. Will you receive it? Can you look beyond what has not happened, what has not been healed or changed, and grab hold of the "Yes Lord," in your spirit? The answer to the will of God is always yes. Did you hear me? The answer to His will in your life for the Generational Revolution is yes and Jesus has given you everything needed to enforce it. It was yes to Abraham when he was still Abram. It was yes to Joseph when he was jailed. Do not let the enemy tell you that the answer must be no because you have not seen it. Your High Priest has heard your petition. Not only that, he put the desire there so that you would ask! And He says,

"Go in Peace – May the God of *(insert your name here)* grant your petition you have made to Him."

CHAPTER 7

The Dead will rise

We are taking a slight detour to address the elephant in the room, the question you have, the thing the enemy keeps telling you as you read this book: "I have done or heard this all before and nothing has changed!" I want to draw your attention to a story that will encourage you in the Book of Ezekiel chapter 37:1-14:

The hand of the Lord was upon me, and carried me out in the spirit of the Lord, and set me down in the midst of the valley which was full of bones,

² And caused me to pass by them round about: and, behold, there were very many in the open valley; and, lo, they were very dry.

³ And he said unto me, Son of man, can these bones live? And I answered, O Lord God, thou knowest.

⁴ Again he said unto me, Prophesy upon these bones, and say unto them, O ye dry bones, hear the word of the Lord.

⁵ Thus saith the Lord God unto these bones; Behold, I will cause breath to enter into you, and ye shall live:

⁶ And I will lay sinews upon you, and will bring up flesh upon you, and cover you with skin, and put breath in you, and ye shall live; and ye shall know that I am the Lord.

⁷ So I prophesied as I was commanded: and as I prophesied, there was a noise, and behold a shaking, and the bones came together, bone to his bone.

⁸ And when I beheld, lo, the sinews and the flesh came up upon them, and the skin covered them above: but there was no breath in them.

⁹ Then said he unto me, Prophesy unto the wind, prophesy, son of man, and say to the wind, Thus saith the Lord God; Come from the four winds, O breath, and breathe upon these slain, that they may live.

¹⁰ So I prophesied as he commanded me, and the breath came into them, and they lived, and stood up upon their feet, an exceeding great army.

¹¹ Then he said unto me, Son of man, these bones are the whole house of Israel: behold, they say, Our bones are dried, and our hope is lost: we are cut off for our parts.

¹² Therefore prophesy and say unto them, Thus saith the Lord God; Behold, O my people, I will open your graves, and cause you to come up out of your graves, and bring you into the land of Israel.

¹³ And ye shall know that I am the Lord, when I have opened your graves, O my people, and brought you up out of your graves,

¹⁴ And shall put my spirit in you, and ye shall live, and I shall place you in your own land: then shall ye know that I the Lord have spoken it, and performed it, saith the Lord. (King James Version)

Let us examine this in sections. The first thing God did was have Ezekiel evaluate the situation. He showed him the condition from every angle. We can say that Ezekiel saw 3 things:

One - They were in an open valley - no protection or covering

Two - from every perspective, the bones were dry, no life

Three - there were a lot of bones

From every perspective, it did not look good. All the evidence showed they were dry bones. However God asked him a question; a question that marks this passage whenever we speak of it -- "Can these bones Live?" Can countless dry bones with no life, in such a low place, and with no protection live? God was asking Ezekiel can the impossible be done with this situation. Ezekiel's answer was classic, "Oh Lord, you know," I believe what Ezekiel meant was, "I don't see a way but if it's your will, nothing is impossible!"

I can imagine the bones were dry because they had been in the valley, or such a low place for very long time! I want you to look at your situation. Can you see the dry bones of life? With every bone it is screaming, "I can't live, it won't work!" With every glance from your eyes, you see death. But we serve a God of the impossible!

Ezekiel was then asked to prophesy (speak a God-inspired word) to the bones. This is what God is saying to you in this book. I know you see your situation as dismal, but the power of God's word is resurrecting it. When you speak the word of God along with Him, together you become a two-edged sword (Hebrews 4:12). The Greek word for two-edged sword in scripture is di-stamos. Di means two and stamos means mouth. This indicates two mouths are speaking. You are one side of the sword and God is on the other. Nothing can stop the sword of the Lord when we speak in faith His resurrecting word over our situations. The dead will rise! God will put sinews and flesh on your situation and breathe life! He is putting it back together again.

The dry bones represented the hope of Israel. It is the hopeless place the enemy constantly drags you to concerning your life. It is the place of faultless lack that tries to permeate your circumstance. The dead situations in your life are rising in victory! The Hannah anointing is being released through this book. Take off the grave clothes of hopelessness and despair. God is blowing His breath of life through this book and is resurrecting your hopes and dreams. You are coming out of the valley of despair into a place of breakthrough!

CHAPTER 8

Activating Your Yes

Can you see yourself as a type of Hannah? Think about your life and trials to see where you fit. You are still here on earth and hoping for change. So, I know you have the same fortitude Hannah had to not give up. Hannah received her yes from the priest and her countenance was changed. Why? Because she believed what Eli said. She trusted Eli. She received the blessing from him. We must do the same with Christ, our High Priest. We need to believe that His yes is yes and that is it. Listen, I understand you may be looking at something that has never changed or could not change in your power. I understand you have gone around this mountain long enough (Deuteronomy 2:3). But the dead things are rising. Hope is no longer deferred! Now what we are going to do is take that yes from our High Priest Jesus, and take steps with a consistent walk of faith.

Step One – Hannah Worshipped. When you believe that God has answered you, you can overrule the burden of the spirit of Peninnah with worship. Instead of being so focused on the thing ahead of you, the thing you have wanted all your life, you can now focus on God. He gets to have your undivided attention and affection. The spirit of Peninnah no longer has power over you. Oh, you may hear the taunts. But it does not affect you as it did and they grow fainter and fainter until you can laugh at the enemy. The place of worship is the place that peace and freedom begin to have full reign. The spirit of

Peninnah wanted to keep you from this freedom. The place of peace and freedom brings power. Remember what Jesus spoke to the storm. He said, "Peace – be still!" (Mark 4:39). With those three powerful words, the storm stopped, and everything came into alignment. Your worship is bringing everything storming against you into alignment. As I am writing this, I see the storm of words over your life, and with every moment you turn your heart in worship to God, the storm begins to calm. Keep worshipping until peace totally reigns and freedom is found in your soul. Worshipping the Father is step one.

Step Two – She went to Ramah. Ramah was the literal place where they lived in Ephraim. It means a hill or high place. Hannah went back to her high place to watch and pray. This is where I know I have missed it so many times in the past. I get the answer, I worship, and I have peace and freedom, then I would just kind of anticipate and wait. While that is a level of faith, what I think we forget about is stewardship. It is important to keep the answer of "yes" in front of you and before the Lord. It is like the story of the 10 talents (Matt 25:14-30). God gave them the yes (talent), but it was up to them to steward what was given. When you steward what is given, Jesus can then give you more. When you don't steward your yes or talent, the consequence is losing what you do have. This is what we do in prayer. This is where strategies may be released and the next steps are given. We are not begging God to do it, we already received it. We are receiving strategies, divine alignment with things and people, or whatever else is needed. Sometimes we just need to sit in our place of prayer and listen. To me, this is the key we miss the most. <u>Often, we put the cart before the horse. Before we even worship and receive freedom from the right now situation, we are already asking for strategy, and the spirit of Peninnah is starting to wear us down again.</u> Make sure you have fully dealt with the accusations in the presence of God before moving onto strategy; or during it, you will be vexed, and your soul sent back to square one. Dealing with accusations may involve repenting, renouncing, and decreeing truth. If you feel yourself becoming anxious and worried, go back to worship and affection, ensure that is good. Then move forward again. It is not in the speed but the consistency.

Step 3 – Putting your faith to action is the final step. Many become stagnate here because they do not see a way, know what to do or do not have the money. Let me say this, sometimes steps 2 and 3 operate together because as you take a step, you need more instruction and prayer. This is perfectly fine, and I assure you God is loving all of this. You are believing His yes and responding! This is how you birth the Generational Revolution!

Putting your faith in action means different things in different situations. There may not be a physical action that you can take. Some actions may involve researching or attaining mentors for the situation. Sometimes simply moving toward the thing in your heart causes doors to open. Above all, be consistent! Decide not to relent until you see the promise.

CHAPTER 9

Birthing a Promise

Let me start by saying, "Yes, you will make it! Yes, you will see the goodness of God in the Land of the Living" (Psalms 27:13). For Hannah and Elkanah to birth a child, they had to be intimate again. . However this time Hannah had her answer and her countenance was changed. Hope was restored and the dry bones didn't look so dry. When they came together in intimacy, God remembered her. I love this word remembered because it means to call to mind or to make mention. I believe the faith actions of Hannah's pursuit caused God to speak over her womb and she conceived. When you have positioned yourself for the birthing through prayer, God will give you the power to conceive (Heb 11:11).

The promise is birthed - Hannah now had a child that was dedicated to the Lord. She weaned him and gave the child to Eli the priest to raise in the fear of God. Your Generational Revolution belongs to God. Ensure you give it entirely to God to do with as He pleases. Abraham finally received his promised son Isaac. He was willing to give Isaac up at the Word of God. Abraham understood that his son was not just for Him, but a seed of purpose for a nation. This mindset helped Abraham to walk by faith concerning his son. Hannah also understood the nature of her promise and was willing to give Samuel to the nations. In doing so, the Israelites lived in peace for many years and received just council and direction from God. I believe Samuel was put on earth to show us how it is possible to live in peace with man and God at the same time. It was not until Israel asked for a king that things begin to shift again. As the "Hannahs'" of the Kingdom of God begin to birth the revolution, I want us to be mindful who it is for. It is not for "your four and no more." It is for the people; and ownership belongs to God. If God asks you to give away or stop doing the thing you feel you were called to, could you? Frequent heart checks are important. Ensure you have people around you who you listen to that have the heart of God for you. Elkanah reminded Hannah to allow God's word to be established. He was there to remind her of the promise and that she should ensure it is fulfilled. Godly council is a good thing to have when you are birthing a Generational Revolutionist.

God has not forgotten you - Just as the blessing is for the generations, it is also for you. Hannah went on to have a total of 7 children. She was able to be the mom she always wanted. Once fruitfulness broke forth in her life, there was no stopping it. The Bible says:

1Sam 2:5 - *They that were* full have hired out themselves for bread; and *they that were* hungry ceased: so that the barren hath born seven; and she that hath many children is waxed feeble. (King James Version)

The spirit of Peninnah had no more power over Hannah. No longer was the barren, barren. Hannah was strong and now producing fruit. This is the reason the enemy is contending in battle so hard for you. Once you produce fruit, you will birth many other things easily to the glory of God!

CHAPTER 10

Are You Ready?

Isaiah 54:1-3 - *Sing, O barren, thou that didst not bear; break forth into singing, and cry aloud, thou that didst not travail with child: for more are the children of the desolate than the children of the married wife, saith the LORD. Enlarge the place of thy tent, and let them stretch forth the curtains of thine habitations: spare not, lengthen thy cords, and strengthen thy stakes; For thou shalt break forth on the right hand and on the left; and thy seed shall inherit the Gentiles, and make the desolate cities to be inhabited.*

Hannahs, God has said yes to what is in you. He had me to write this book to admonish you to move forward. I know it may have been painful and long. I know you may have felt you have tried everything. But I am admonishing you to cast your net again on the ground of His word. You see, you have been in a process. This process has brought you to a place of being totally sold out to God. You are now willing to give everything back to Him for His good pleasure. It has not been without pain or without suffering. But what you are producing is Generational. You were put on the earth for the end time. You were put here to do something no one has ever seen. So, in case you did not know it, look around – you are up next! You are prepared, you are equipped, and you have everything you need in Him. The Generations are waiting for the answer God has given you. We need you to take step into faith and go forth with the eyes of His Word.

Hannahs, ALL the pain is bringing great joy.

God has exalted your horn (Psalms 92:10), and is bringing you higher! Sing the song of peace and dance the dance of victory! Enlarge the place of your tent (Isaiah 54:2). This is your mindset to receive all that God has through the word. Prepare your heart and soul to say, "I know it's beyond me, but yes!" The verse above says, "spare not". Do not hold back in faith and vision. Do not let fear and the spirit of Peninnah cripple you anymore. Move forward with the Hannah Anointing!

You are Hannah. You are one who perseveres in prayer. You remember you are one that watches with God, to win every battle. You are one who does not allow what has happen to be your height in life. You defeat the Spirit of Peninnah that has tried to vex you and keep you down. You will give birth to a generational revolution. You will break into fruitfulness.

You are Hannah!

#IAMHANNAH

CLOSING PRAYER

My Father, thank you for loving me and allowing me to pick up this book. By faith, I receive this word. I surrender my life to your will. I know you have plans to prosper me, to give me a hope and a future (Jeremiah 29:11). Because of this, I am willing to be a Generational Revolutionist for the next generation. I say, "yes to your will. I will receive the promise!" Every spirit of Peninnah is broken off my life! I receive the love of my Father once and for all. I trust His way and I move into my season by faith. Every power operating in my life is drowned by the Spirit of God. The word overwhelms the voice of the enemy. The word thunders over my life (Job 37:2 NLT) and shakes the wicked out of it. My promise are here and now. My seed of breakthrough will perpetuate throughout all generations. Christ in me, the hope of glory causes me to triumph. I will arise as a Hannah and see the goodness of the lord in the land of the living.